978 0956 6014 07

What lies within the
Colliery Days
Fabric Project Book

Concentration Level

◯ Nice and relaxing... let's day dream

◯◯ This is fun

◯◯◯ Mmmm, let's think

◯◯◯◯ Put the coffee on, white no sugar

Florrie

Favourite things
Chocolate, Collies and Old Quilts

Favourite Past time
Sewing and more Sewing

Favourite Flower
Alliums

Silliest Job
Willick Pin Polisher (Cullercoats)

Best Memory
Riding me bike down Horatio Street, Newcastle to get Ice Cream (I'm partial to a Tutti Fruiti)

Betty

Favourite things
Notebooks, Musicals and Bumble Bees

Favourite Past time
Singing – Loudly!

Favourite Flower
Scented Sweet Peas

Silliest Job
Fadge Kneader (Village Bakery)

Best Memory
Sitting in dappled sunlight and listening to the band on a beautiful summers day

The Scullery & Kitchen

**Oh aye....
when I was
only knee high
I remember the
smells of Ma
cooking in
the kitchen**

Mother would get up and start cooking, she used to bake... nearly every day she used to do that.

The washing, well, she used to boil the clothes in a great big pan. Now when I think about it you can hardly realise how she could lift it. It was full of water and when it wasn't in use for to boil the clothes, she used it as a bread bin and it was full of loaves of bread.

florrie

Crazy Patchwork Tea Cosy

A main feature in every cottage is the best Tea Cosy. We have made ours using a favourite technique of the time, crazy patchwork.

What you need

Assorted fabrics
12 x 6½" squares

Fusible wadding
(H640) 40cms (16")

Lining fabric 30cms (12")

Freezer paper

Optional

Lace or ribbons

Threads

Finished Size: 13" x 8½" approx

How to make it

Place your fabric squares into 3 stacks of 4 fabrics, right sides up. Put a freezer paper template from page 54, on the top of each pile and iron in place. **See photo.** On one of the stacks, with a ruler and rotary cutter (or you can use scissors) cut on the centre line, and separate into 2 halves. **See photo.** Cut on the remaining lines.

To mix the fabrics up do not touch fabric A. Put the first B fabric on the stack to the bottom of its stack. Stack C take the top 2 fabrics keeping them together and put them to the bottom of the stack. Stack D, take the top 3 fabrics and put to the bottom of the stack. Continue with each fabric in the block in the same manner.

When sewing the block together do not worry too much about matching the seams perfectly as they will be trimmed later.

Sew the left hand side of the block first. Put fabric A & B RST, sew. Following the pattern add fabric C. Now sew the right hand side of the block fabrics D & E RST and add fabric F. Sew the right and left sides together and trim to a 5" square.

Repeat until all 12 blocks are completed.

Take 6 of the blocks and sew together in 2 rows of 3. **See photo.**

Place on top of the H640 wadding and embellish as desired. Repeat with the remaining 6 blocks. **See photo on page 6.**

Make a template from page 59, with freezer paper and using it as a guide cut out a front and back of the tea cosy.

Place these RST and sew around the curved edge. If you want to, insert lace and ribbon before you sew the curved edge.

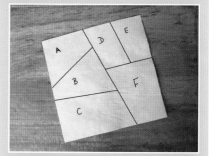

Using the same template cut out 2 pieces from the lining fabric. Sew around the curved edge.

Turn lining pieces to the right side and place inside the outside pieces matching the side seams. Sew around the bottom edge leaving a 3" gap to turn through.

After turning through, either slip stitch the opening closed or turn in the fabric and top stitch near to the bottom edge.

Canny Pot Holder

We have carried on the 'crazy theme' with this glove shaped pot holder for the range. For those of us who are not lucky enough to own a range, this pot holder looks just as good in a contemporary kitchen.

Ginger Nut Biscuits

In a bowl put

1lb of flour

Half an ounce of ground ginger

A teaspoon of Bicarbonate of Soda

A pinch of all spice

A pinch of salt

Half a pint of treacle

2 ounces of butter

Mix all the ingredients together to form a stiff paste. Divide into two dozen pieces and roll each piece with the palm of your hand until they are the size of a small egg.

Pop on a greased baking tray, 2" apart.

Place into a hot oven and cook for 15 minutes. Use the Canny Pot Holder to remove the gorgeous biscuits from the oven.

Betty

What you need

Assorted fabrics 6 x 6½" squares

Fusible wadding (H640) 40cms (16")

Binding & loop fabric 10cms (4")

Lining fabric 40cms (16")

Freezer paper

Optional

Threads

Finished Size: 10½" x 7½" approx

Cutting

1 strip 10" x 2" for loop

1 strip 2¼" x 16½" for binding

How to make it

Follow the Tea Cosy instructions and make 6 of the crazy blocks. Sew them together in 2 rows of 3, embelish as required. **See photo on page 4.**

Make a template from page 59, with freezer paper and using it as a guide cut out the front of the pot holder from the crazy panel.

Place the backing fabric on top of the wadding and quilt as desired. We quilted a grid of 2" squares. Using the template cut out the backing piece of the pot holder.

Place the sides RST and sew around the curved edge.

Using the same template cut out 2 pieces from the lining fabric. Sew around the curved edge.

Turn lining pieces to the right side, and place inside the outside pieces matching the side seams.

Sew the long edge of the loop fabric and turn through. Centre the seam to the back and press. Fold in half and position the raw edges to the straight edge of the pot holder (fold of loop pointed towards the curved edge).

Bind the bottom of the pot holder incorporating the loop. Bind in your preferred method or see the Work Basket for our method.

LOOP

Proggy Tea Pot Stand

Grandpa's New Rug

When I was a little girl
I loved to wrap up snug
In Grandpa's big
old comfy chair
And watch him make a rug

Betty

Every cottage has several 'Proggy' or 'Hooky' mats.

We have taken the flower from one particular mat and made a Proggy Tea Pot stand, our nod to this beautiful art work. Making mats was an important part of family life, with everybody joining in, cutting the fabrics, designing the patterns and making the rugs.

What you need

Brown fabric 30cm (12")

Pink fabric 30cm (12")

Cream fabric 30cm (12")

Scrap of red fabric

Hessian, Fat quarter

Embroidery/Quilt hoop

Proggy tool

Freezer paper

Finished Size: 7" x 7" approx

Cutting Recipe

Cut all of the fabrics into 2¾" strips

Sub cut into ¾" pieces

How to make it

Draw a 7" x 7" square in the centre of your Hessian.

Now add a 2" border to all 4 sides of this square. This will be your cutting line when you have completed the proggy mat.

Trace the template of the flower on page 60 onto the freezer paper and cut it out. Place this flower into the centre of the 7" square and draw around it. Draw the flower centre freehand.

Centre Hessian in the hoop.

It is important to work in lines.

Start at the bottom right hand side if you are right handed, or the left if you are left handed of the 7" square.

Poke the proggy tool into the Hessian and push through one end of a piece of fabric and pull it through from the underneath to approximately half way.

Make another hole next to the first one and push down the other end of the fabric.

Pull both ends under the Hessian so they are tight and even. **See photos.**

Continue across the row, tightly covering the design and following the colours as per the photograph.

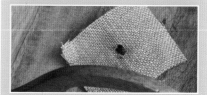

Once completed remove from the hoop and cut on the cutting line previously drawn.

The back of a proggy is the flat side

Fold and neaten the edges to the back of the proggy and sew using a whip stitch.

BRIEF HISTORY OF PROGGY

They say the Vikings originally brought over the first examples of the proggy mat, which is now synonymous to the North East.

Proggy mats were a common sight in working-class homes and Colliery Villages in the North East of England until the mid-20th Century.

Made from old sacks and recycled fabric they were an economical option to keep feet warm and toasty in an era before fitted carpets were the norm.

The basic requirements were a frame and a hook or progger which were made by the local men. The backing material was hessian, from old sacks. The 'cloots' to be cut into clippings for the mat came from 'aad claes' (old clothes), long past handing down to younger family members. Trousers, jackets and coats made from hardwearing tweeds or worsteds were best, navy blue, black or brown were the commonest colours available.

WARNIN THIEVES T ALLOTM GARDE

A spate of recen have let to loca warning reside Pitfield Street t they keep a wa gardens.

Prize leeks wer from Miss Flor garden during t of June 30th wl Florrie was visi friend in the ne Broad beans pla stripped bare in garden belongin Betty, who is sa 'very cross' abc whole episode. Police urge resi to keep an eye vegetables and them if they kn the culprits are. Biff is keeping

Skinny Winnie Doll

Winnie is a fabulous long skinny doll, dressed for a day's hard work. Laundry was a prominent part of the day and Winnie is ready for it in her long waisted pinny. Inspired by archive photographs of weekly wash days and the baskets of washing she is absolutely charming!

Rub a Dub Dub

The bubbles are tippling
out of the tub
I haven't got time to play
I've possed and I've mangled
with a rub a dub dub
It's another washing day

I'm really very tired
I've been washing all day long
The claes are clean and ready
To go back where they belong

Betty

What you need

Tea dyed calico 25cms (10")

Fabric for dress 50cms (20")

Petticoat 35cms (14")

Apron 35cms (14")

Dolls hair

Toy filling

Freezer paper

Dark brown acrylic paint (optional)

Elastic (narrow) 7" length

Pigma Pen

Finished size: 24" high approx

How to make it

Make the body first

Fold the calico in half with RST. Make freezer paper templates of the arms, body & legs on page 59, transfer all markings from the templates.

Using the templates as a guide, sew around each piece leaving an opening for turning through as indicated on the pattern.

It is better to reduce the stitch length on your machine, as this will make the body stronger and minimise the toy filling escaping.

Use pinking shears to cut out the pieces.

Stuff legs, arms and body firmly to the lines indicated on the pattern.

When stuffing the pieces do not be tempted to put a large piece of toy filling in at once. You will achieve a smoother finish if you insert the toy filling in smaller amounts.

Before attaching the legs turn the raw edge of the body under ¼" and finger press. Place the legs inside the body and stitch opening closed, ensuring the legs are firmly sewn in place.

Turn in the raw edges of each arm and sew the arms in place on each shoulder.

Mark where you want the shoes to be on the legs. Use a pencil and paint them dark brown & let them dry.

It is better to apply several light layers of paint, allowing them to dry in between rather than putting too much paint on your brush.

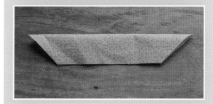

Continued

Skinny Winnie Doll

Hard work, was washing day!

They had an old fashioned washer and a big mangle, I was used with them because mother had them. You had to turn this great big iron wheel and inside it was wood, just like those little cages you see the mice in, but it was huge and it fitted in the washer. You talk about the heat, what with the fire being on boiling the clothes and turning the wheel, the sweat was just coming out of you. I did all the housework, for all she had a rougher bringing up than me, she liked to act the lady, she was the manager's wife and she let people see that.

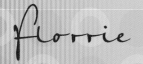

To make the Petticoat

Cut the fabric 12½" x 23" and hem the bottom.

Turn under the top of the petticoat ½" and sew to create a casing for the elastic.

Sew the short sides RST, and turn through. Pin the elastic onto a safety pin and thread it through the casing. Remove the safety pin and join the elastic by tying a small knot. The size will be adjusted when you dress Winnie. **See photo on page 10.**

To make the Dress

See Bodice template on page 59. Cut out 2 on fold of fabric.

With RST sew from sleeve edge to neck opening.

Cut 2 x skirt pieces 15" x 13".

Hem one long side of each piece, (front and back) this is the bottom of the skirt. Gather the top of each piece with a small running stitch until they match the bodice.

Pin one of the skirt pieces RST to the front of the bodice and repeat for the back and sew in place.

Starting at the bottom of the sleeve, sew the side seams and turn them through. **See photo on page 10.**

Sew a running stitch around the bottom edge of each sleeve, this will be gathered & tied after the dress is placed on the doll.

To make the Pinny

Cut a piece of fabric 12½" x 16".

Hem the two short sides and one long side. Gather the unsewn edge to measure 6½".

To make the apron strings, cut a piece of fabric 2½" x 22". Fold in half RST.

Mark a 45 degree angle at each end and cut fabric. **See photo on page 10.**

Sew around all sides leaving a gap for turning. Now turn through.

Centre the apron strings onto the pinny RST and sew in place.

Dress the doll.

To make the Hair

It is better to do the hair before the face.

Put two pins in the head for the eye placement. Place 6 pins in the head. **See Photo.**

Wrap the hair around the pins until the head is covered, and sew in place. Remove pins.

Using a Pigma Pen draw in the eyes, and use blusher for rosy cheek features.

Winnie looks lovely displayed sitting down, however if you use a doll stand, the full effect of the apron is visible.

If you wish to hang the doll on a wall, simply add a button to her upper back, then either hang by a cord or on one of the rustic hangers available in your local quilt shop.

Colliery Peg Bag

Lucky that shoe missed us

I had a boyfriend when I lived at C Pit, he was ginger. We went to play in the coal house and we used to get on top, because I was a right tomboy, and this was a Sunday with me best frock on... me best frock was blue serge with smocking in red, it had long sleeves and I hated them... here, I fell through the top and I was hanging by me ears, the coal had got low and I thought that me feet would touch it but here, I was hanging by me ears. Never mind they got us out but I'd clicked my good Sunday frock. Me mother never hit us and I can remember it as if it were today, I walked in the back end and she took off her shoe and let bleeze and it missed us. I never heard the last of that.

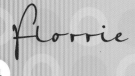

14

In a dresser in one of the Colliery Cottages, the shelves are edged with newspapers cut into patterns. One of them is an unusual hexagonal shape with a heart detail, this inspired us to create this peg bag.

What you need

Main fabric 50cms (20")

Co-ordinating fabric Fat 8th

Calico 40cms (16")

3 buttons

Heat 'n' Bond Ultra

Freezer paper

Threads

Coat hanger

Finished Size: 16" x 11" approx

How to make it

Make 3 templates A, B and C from page 60 using freezer paper.

From the main fabric cut out a Template A and C.

From the co-ordinating fabric cut out Template B.

From the calico, cut Templates A, B and C.

Lay all three fabrics on top of the calico matching sizes, WST and pin in place.

On pieces A and B hem the long edges.

Make tabs by cutting 2 strips 10" x 3" from the main fabric, fold in half RST and sew down the long edge. Turn through and press the seam to the back. Fold in half and position onto the right side of piece C, refer to template C for placement.

Place piece B RST onto piece C (at the top) and then place piece A on top RST (at the bottom).

Pieces A and B will overlap, this stops your pegs from falling out. **See photo.**

Sew around the outer edges and turn through.

Using Heat 'n' Bond Ultra trace the heart on page 60 and fuse into place. **See photo.**

Make 3 Yo-Yo's using the template on page 58. See the Work Basket for instructions. Sew into place adding a button. **See photo.**

Add coat hanger.

Florrie has made this bag using a plastic coated fabric (aye hinny an oil cloth), she wanted hers to be waterproof.

Father's Keepy Back Cushion

Inspired by the wages tins and miners' lamps, this cushion is a simple striped design but with a hidden pocket. Keepy backs are monies put to one side often without 'wor lass' knowing, used to subsidise trips to the football, dogs or a liquid refreshments establishment! With an appliqué of a miner's lamp this is a fun cushion to make. Change the lamp for a corsage and you have Mother's Keepy Back cushion!

C Pit Poem

The Miners go down
the pit each day
It's the only way to
earn some pay
With cupboards to fill and
children to keep
Very little money and
not much sleep

They go deep down to the
bowels of the earth
Let us show some respect and
know their worth
When you sit by the fire,
dreaming sweet dreams
Remember the men,
at the dark coal seams

Betty

What you need

Fabrics

6 x 2 ½" strips WOF (Ideal for Jelly Roll)

Fabric for pocket 9 ½" x 9 ½" square

Binding 10cms (4")

Scrap of black fabric for Appliqué

Heat 'n' Bond Ultra

14" cushion pad

Finished Size: 14" x 14" approx

How to make it

Join all of the 2 ½" strips together to create a long thin piece of fabric.

Cut into seven 2½" x 34" lengths.

Arrange in a pleasing manner and sew them together along the 34" length.

You should now have a panel measuring 14½" x 34".

Make a double hem on one of the short edges. Press and stitch to secure.

Now make the pocket. Hem 2 opposite sides of the pocket fabric and stitch in place.

Fold the fabric in half RST, stitch down each short side. Turn through and press.

Take the cushion panel and position your pocket on the wrong side of the panel, with the folded edge of the pocket in line with the raw edge.

Bind the edge making sure the pocket is sewn into the binding. **See photo.**

Measure 10" up from the pocket edge of the cushion panel and mark with a pin.

Measure 24" from the pocket edge of the cushion panel and mark with another pin.

With RST fold the pocket end of the cushion panel on the 10" mark, pin in place.

Fold the opposite end on the 24" mark. You should now have an overlap of approximately 4".

Sew down each side and turn through.

Trace the miners lamp from page 63 onto the Heat 'n' Bond Ultra and fuse into place. **See photo for placement.**

Insert cushion pad.

Slang Hangings

The North East of England has its own unique dialects and words. These add to the colour and interest of the people and places.

Our 3 hangings Netty, Canny and Hinny capture a small part of it.

The Colliery Rows had their outside 'Netties' (lavatories), the people are 'Canny' (nice) and if they refer to you as 'Hinny' it's a term of endearment.

Betty's Netty Paper

Take several pages of the 'Chronicle', not today's!

Tear into pieces about 7" by 5".

Pile them together and using a large needle and some string, sew them together to form a loop.

Hang the loop on the back of the Netty door.

Use when ready.

Betty

What you need

For one hanging

Neutral fabric Fat 16th

Backing fabric Fat 16th

Wadding Fat 16th

Binding fabric 1 strip 1¾" x WOF

Fabric for Appliqué assorted scraps

Heat 'n' Bond Ultra

Embroidery thread

2 buttons

Jute string 16"

Finished Size: 9" x 7" approx

Cutting Recipe

Neutral fabric 9" x 7"

Backing fabric 9" x 7"

Wadding 9" x 7"

Binding fabric 4 x 1¾" strips

How to make it

Choose your hanging from the templates on page 54, 55, 61.

For each hanging it is easier if you trace the 'definitions' of your chosen saying first onto the Neutral fabric. **See photo for placement.**

Fuse the letters as per instructions in the Work Basket on page 56. **See photo for placement.**

Place the wadding onto the back of the neutral fabric and using 2 strands of embroidery thread stitch the words through the fabric and wadding. We used a back stitch and french knots.

Add the backing fabric and bind the hanging (see the Work Basket for our method).

Sew a button in each of the two top corners.

Tie the ends of the string around the buttons.

You are now ready to hang up your sign.

The Bedroom & Parlour

I used to love afternoon tea with Ma's freshly baked cakes

Little cakes

2oz self raising flour

2oz caster sugar

2oz margarine

1 egg

Heat the oven to 190°c. Beat the egg senseless! Pop the margarine and sugar into a bowl and cream together until light and fluffy. Add the poor little egg and the sieved flour a little at a time beating well.

Put spoonfuls of the mixture into bun cases. Bake for 15 minutes until golden brown and well risen.

Fill your boots!

Betty

Pitfield Street Quilts

The Pitfield Street Quilts are great beginners quilts. The design was inspired by the stone floors in the Colliery Rows and the appliqué from the buildings in the Colliery Village. Simple but very effective!

The quilt can be made with or without the appliqué. The lap quilt is a smaller version of the quilt and is ideal for snuggling up on a cold night.

Aye quilting was a life saver for us

Aye quilting was a life saver for us. When me father was finished at the pit we had to move in with my sister and her man further along the row. Mam and my older sisters would make quilts on the evenings and weekends to keep the family.

What you need

Pitfield Street Quilt

28 x Assorted fabrics
6½" x 42" WOF

Top border fabric
10cms (4" WOF)

Binding fabric
60cms (24")

Appliqué background fabric 60cms (24" WOF)

Heat 'n' Bond Lite

Threads to match

Assorted fabrics for Appliqué

Wadding 2.5m (96")

Backing fabric
2m (78") 108" wide fabric

Lap Quilt

10 x Assorted fabrics
6½" x 42" WOF

Backing 2.8m (112")

Wadding 1.5m (60")

Binding 35cms (14")

Pitfield Street Quilt

**Finished Size with appliqué:
70" x 88" approx**

**Finished Size without appliqué:
70" x 76" approx**

Cutting Recipe

From 12 of your strips cut a 6½" x 4½" rectangle. These are your half rectangles. You require 12 half rectangles in total. Cut the remaining part of these strips into 6½" x 8½" rectangles.

Cut the rest (16 strips) into 6½" x 8½" rectangles. You will need a total of 111 full rectangles.

From the appliqué background fabric cut 2 x 10½" strips WOF.

Top border cut 2 x 1½" strips WOF.

Binding strips cut 9 x 2¼" strips WOF.

How to Make it

Because this is a scrap quilt you can either plan the placement of your fabrics, or you can place them randomly, it is up to you.

Continued

Pitfield Street Quilts

Adopted Geordies

Mam and Dad came up from Lancashire to work in the pits. Mam was really chapel she loved it, she used to be part of the sewing circle.

Never mind, they made lovely quilts and they were auctioned for to get money.

Florrie

In row one sew 9 of the full rectangles together.

In row two start with a half rectangle, then add 8 full rectangles and finish with another half rectangle.

Repeat rows 1 & 2 until you have completed 13 rows in total. You must finish with a row 1 so the top and bottom rows of the quilt only contain full rectangles.

Sew the rows together.

If you are adding the appliqué sew the top border strip to top of quilt.

Appliqué

Sew together background strips of fabric.

Refer to the photo on page 23 for placement of the appliqué pieces. We used the school, two pit cottages, the pit head, and the chapel. See the templates in the Work Basket on pages 55, 57, 63. Appliqué as per instructions in the Work Basket. You can embellish and embroider the buildings by hand or use your sewing machine. **See photos** for some ideas and inspiration.

When the appliqué is completed sew the finished strip to the top of the quilt.

Layer up quilt, and quilt as desired.

Bind your quilt using your preferred method or see our method in the Work Basket.

Lap Quilt

Finished Size: 48" x 52" approx

Cutting Recipe

From 8 of your strips cut a 4½" x 8½" rectangle, these are your half rectangles. You require 8 half rectangles in total. Cut the remaining part of these strips into 6½" x 8½" rectangles.

Cut the remaining 2 strips into 6½" x 8½" rectangles. You will need a total of 50 full rectangles.

How to

Our lap quilt consists of 9 rows with 6 full rectangles in row 1.

However you can make this quilt whatever size you wish, and even add some appliqué to the top, the choice is yours.

Refer to the large quilt instructions for completion.

Florrie's tip

We have left 2" gaps between our appliquéd buildings on the large quilt.

If you decide to use a different combination of buildings for your quilt, I would suggest that you place them on the top of the background fabric until you are happy with the arrangement and gaps, before you fix them permanently into place.

Draught Excluder

It was never nice going for coal especially in the winter

The rows were cold places until the fire got started. I would help Mam and Dad by going for coal; I used to gan to the coal heaps and put the coal on a bogie made from old mangle wheels.

florrie

The Colliery Cottages were dependant on the range for warmth, so items that helped the families keep warm were very useful. This is a lovely big draught excluder incorporating the appliqué from the 'Pitfield Street Quilt'.

Our excluder is firmly stuffed to give it weight, however if you wanted to make yours into a long cushion for a settle or sofa, a little less stuffing would be ideal.

What you need

Fabric for background, backing & gussets 85cms (34")	Toy filling
Assorted fabrics for Appliqué	**Optional**
	Buttons
Heat 'n' Bond Lite	Threads

Finished Size: 32" x 13" approx

Cutting Recipe

From the main fabric cut 2 pieces for the front & back two x 12½" x 32½"

Gussets; two x 3" x 33" and two x 3" x 13"

How to make it

Using the templates on pages 55, 57, 63, choose which designs you want on your draught excluder. We used the school, a pit cottage row and the pit head.

Appliqué these onto the front panel using your preferred method or see our Work Basket.

Embellish the panel at this stage.

To construct the excluder, sew the two long gusset pieces to the top and bottom of your front panel RST, ensuring you have a ¼" overlap at each end. (This makes joining easier).

Now sew the short gusset pieces to the side of the front panel RST.

Match the gusset seams and sew in place.

Take the backing fabric and pin to the gusset RST, please take care to match the corners.

Sew in place leaving a 4" gap. Turn through and stuff firmly. Hand sew the opening closed.

Betty made the appliqué front panel of the draught excluder, into a delightful wall hanging.

Bed or Table Runner

A lovely star inspired runner for either your bed or table, this piece is a delight. We were thinking about the work people of this period undertook and how hard life was. A good nights sleep would have been a luxury and a blessing. We incorporated a star into the design because in our eyes, the people were stars and many stars can be found in the quilts and flooring of this period.

What you need

Fabric A: Centre square 15cms (6" WOF)

Fabric B: Cream corner square 10cms (4")

Fabric C: Large cream triangles 20cms (8")

Fabric D: Large pink triangles 80cms (32")

Fabric E: Small dark red triangles 20cms (8")

Setting and corner triangles 1.10m (44")

Binding fabric 35cms (14")

Wadding 60cms (24") 90" wide

Backing fabric 60cms (24") 108" wide fabric

Finished Size: 17¾" x 88" approx

Cutting Recipe

Fabric A: Cut 1 x 4½" strip WOF and sub cut into 5 x 4½" squares

Fabric B: Cut 3 x 3½" strips WOF and sub cut into 20 x 3½" squares

Fabric C: Cut 1 x 7¼" strips and sub cut into 5 x 7¼" squares

Cut twice diagonally to make 4 triangles

Fabric D: Cut 1 x 7¼" strip WOF and sub cut into 5 x 7¼" squares

Cut each square twice diagonally to make 4 triangles

Fabric E: Cut 1 x 3⅞" strip WOF and sub cut each into 10 x 3⅞" squares

Cut once on diagonal to make 2 triangles

Setting triangles: Cut 2 x 13⅞" strips WOF and sub cut into 6 x 13⅞"

Cut each one once on the diagonal to make 2 triangles

Corner triangles: Cut 1 x 12" square WOF and sub cut into 2 x 12" squares

Cut once on diagonal to make 2 triangles

Binding strips cut 6 x 2¼" strips WOF

How to make it

To complete one block, sew an E triangle to a B square and then add a D triangle to the long edge. **See photo.** Make 4 of these units.

Referring to the main photo sew a unit to either side of fabric A. This forms the middle row of the block.

The remaining 2 units sew a Fabric C triangle to each side. **See photo.**

Carefully matching seams sew these units to either side of the middle row.

The block is now completed and should measure 12½" square. Make a total of 5 blocks.

Lay the 5 blocks on point and add the setting triangles. It is useful to lay them out prior to sewing them together; this ensures that you sew the setting triangle along the correct edge.

Stitch the rows together and lastly add the corner triangles.

Layer up runner, and quilt as desired.

Bind your runner using your preferred method or see our method in the Work Basket binding instructions.

To make a table runner, adjust the number of blocks to the size of your table.

29

NEED HELP?

To complete one block. Sew an E triangle to a B square and then add a D triangle to the long edge. See below.

CHAPE...
HOL...
STRAWBER...

A Strawberry F...
taking place at...
Methodist Chap...
It will take plac...
church hall on S...
July 31st. Door...
be open all day...
refreshments w...
provided by the...
Sewing Circle....
Strawberries w...
with a sprinklin...
for a farthing....
Miss Betty is ru...
a craft table to...
funds for the ch...
all contribution...
be taken to the...
Friday evening....
Entertainment v...
pr... N...

Merry Go Round Cushion

Fun at the Hoppin's

*When the Hoppin's
(Newcastle Temperance
Festival) came I loved it.
Mam would pack us up some
homemade bread and jam
and some little cakes she
made (best bit for me was
she'd let me lick the bowl).
Aye, we had a canny time,
games, competitions and
loads of entertainment.*

A lovely circular stitchery cushion encapsulating,
Merry Go Round horses and stylised shuggy boats.

Life was hard in the mining villages, domestic work was labour
intensive and the mine work dirty, back breaking and dangerous.
When the fair came to town it spelt fun with a capital 'F'.

What you need

Stitchery panel

Background fabric Fat quarter

Embroidery thread

Weaveline Fat quarter

Fabric for piping, & backing
50cms (20")

Gusset fabric 20cms (8")

Half inch piping cord
54½"

Round cushion pad
17" diameter

Hera Marker

Finished Size: 17" approx

Cutting Recipe

Gusset, cut 2 x 3½" strips
to make a 54½" length

Piping, cut 1¾" strips on bias
to make a total of 54½" length

How to make it

Place weaveline to the reverse of the
background fabric. Trace the pattern from
page 62, 63 onto the fabric. Using 2 strands
of embroidery thread backstitch the design,
adding french knots for the horses eyes.

Make a circle template from freezer paper
17" in diameter and place it over the
stitchery ensuring it is in the centre. Using
the template as a guide cut it out.

Check the circumference of your stitchery
circle now to ensure that it measures 52". If
it does not, do not panic adjust the piping
and gusset.

Cut the template in half. Fold the backing
fabric in half and place cut template
4½" down from the fold. Straight edges
matching.

Cut around the curve, and then cut in half
along the fold.

Along the straight edges of each backing
piece, using a Hera Marker, mark 2 lines at
a ¼" and a ½". Fold these over to make a
hem and stitch in place.

Join ends together to make a circle.

Place the piping cord down the centre of
the wrong side of the fabric. Pin and tack
close to the cord. **See photo.**

Pin and tack the piping cord RST onto the
front of the cushion.

Sew the gusset fabric into a circle and sew
RST to the front of the cushion. Sew very
close to the piping cord, the zipper foot or
piping foot on your machine is very useful.

Pin the 2 backing pieces RST to the gusset,
there will be an overlap on the backing
pieces. Sew in place. Turn the cushion
through and insert a cushion pad.

**This stitchery looks equally good as a
square cushion or a simple wall hanging.**

Floral Frame

The Colliery Rows are heavily decorated inside with pictures and frames, the walls are covered with delicate floral papers. We have combined the two to make an embellished floral frame. Very pretty!

What you need

2 x Fat 8ths of Co-ordinating fabrics	Wadding scraps
1 x Fat 16th of a plain fabric	Embroidery thread
	Buttons
Scraps of fabric for 3D flowers	Heat 'n' Bond Ultra
	Glue gel
Grey board 2 pieces 7" x 9"	Bookbinding glue
	Craft knife

Finished Size: 7" x 9" approx

Cutting Recipe

Cut the two Fat 8ths into 2 separate pieces measuring 9½" x 11½"

Cut the Fat 16th into a piece measuring 8¾" x 6¾"

On one of the grey board pieces measure 1½" in from the edge on all sides, and mark the aperture

Cut out this middle section with a craft knife. **See photo**

Cut the wadding into 1½" x 9" strips You will need approximately 12

How to make it

The frame is constructed first and then the 3D flowers attached.

The frame

Take the uncut grey board, (this is the back of the frame), and cover with one of the 9½" x 11" pieces of fabric. Turn the edges over and glue into place using bookbinding glue.

On the side with the folded edges, glue the 8¾" x 6¾" piece of fabric (this covers up the rough edges).

Take the aperture grey board and cover one side of the frame completely with the 3 layers of wadding. Sticking them in place with bookbinding glue.

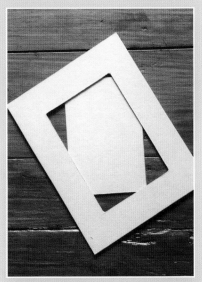

Continued

Floral Frame

My Floral Frame

Here I sit upon the floor
Surrounded by beautiful
fabrics galore
There are rosebuds, stripes
and big fat spots
Circles, checks and tiny dots
I really can't have two
the same
For when I make my
floral frame

Betty

Place the last piece of fabric right side down on the table.

Position the aperture frame in the centre of the fabric (wadding side down).

With a pencil draw around the aperture and remove the frame.

Measure 1" in from these marks and then cut out the smaller drawn aperture.

Cut diagonals into the corners of the fabric to allow it to fold easily.

Place the aperture back on the wrong side of the fabric and turn in the outer edges (folding the corners in first and then the sides to make a mitred corner). Secure with bookbinding glue. **See photo on page 32.**

Fold in the inner edges and secure with the bookbinding glue, (put a little glue in the corners to stop any fraying).

Allow to dry.

Take the back of the frame and with the plain fabric facing you, glue the top aperture on to it on three edges only, using glue gel. (Do not glue the top edge this is where your photo will slot in). Allow to dry.

3D flowers

Trace 4 of each flower onto Heat 'n' Bond Ultra. See page 55, 56.

Fuse 2 large and 2 small flowers onto two different fabrics.

Peel off the backing and iron all the flowers onto a third fabric.

For each small flower pinch a petal together and secure with a stitch. **See photo.**

Pinch alternate petals and repeat.

Position the small flowers onto the large flowers, **see photo on page 33.** Secure the two together by sewing on a small button.

Using glue gel, glue the flowers onto the frame and allow to dry thoroughly overnight would be ideal.

Florrie's tips

These little frames can be made with or without the flowers. Try a plaid or stripe for a boy's room, pastel or primary colours would suit a nursery and homespun fabrics give a canny country look.

The flowers can be added to other decorative items. Three dimensional, they can be added to a bag or doll. Leaving them one dimensional add them to a notebook or decoupage them onto cards.

Lets decorate the world kiddas!

Ma's Special Things

I wear glasses now, me Ma might have been right

I loved to make things when I was a lass and I was egged on with it...

When I used to do it by the lamplight, I remember me Ma saying...

'You'll suffer for that'.

Florrie

Mother's Posh Bag

Sunday Best

Mother always wanted
A beautiful posh handbag
She had to save up very hard
After seeing the huge price tag!

It came out every Sunday
As off to chapel she went
She felt like a queen
All posh and serene
And considered
       it money well spent

Betty

Inspired by the shapes of the bags hanging on the bedstead, we have designed a lovely bag for todays woman. A beautiful quilted handbag, a bit more posh than the usual fabric bag!

What you need

Handles

Fabric for top band & loops 30cm (12")

Lining fabric 50cm (20")

Fabric for bias 41"

505 basting spray

Fabric for main bag 50cm (20")

Fusible wadding (H640) 30cm (12")

Freezer paper

Thread to match fabrics

Finished Size:
10" x 14" approx without handles

Cutting Recipe

Top band of bag 26½" x 5"

Fusible wadding (H640) 26½" x 2"

Fabric for lower section of bag. 2 pieces of both, outside & lining 10½" x 14½"

Fusible wadding (H640) 10½" x 14½"

Bias strips of fabric for the interior of bag 1" strips WOF

Fabric for loops 4 x 5½" x 1½"

How to make it

The bag is constructed in two parts which are then joined together.

To make the lower part of the bag

Fuse the wadding to the reverse of the outside fabric, and spray baste the reverse of the lining to the other side of the wadding.

Quilt the fabrics as desired, using threads that match the fabrics.

Using the freezer paper make a template of the bag, see page 56. Transfer all markings on template. Iron the template onto the quilted fabric, cut out.

Make the two darts in the bottom of the bag by pinning points A to B, and then sew from point C to AB.

Pin and baste the gathers on the top by matching points D to E and F to G.

Put the bag pieces RST pin and sew around the curved edge.

Make the bias strips and use to cover the inside seams.

Top band of the bag

Iron the fabric in half WST, open it up and iron the wadding in the middle. Turn the edges of the fabric in by ¼" and sew around the three open ends close to the edge. Quilt the band as desired. Sew the short ends together to form a circle.

Make 4 loops to attach the handles. Take the fabric & fold in half lengthwise, sew together & turn through.

Position handles **see photo**. Matching the seams pin & sew the top band of the bag to the base of the bag. **See photo.**

Neaten the seam with bias strips as before and hand sew the loops to the top band. This stops them moving around.

Big, Beautiful & Bold Corsages

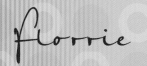
Floral patterns were prominent in the cottages, the walls, fabrics, rugs and many other items in the Colliery Village. Inspiration for our Corsages has been taken from the fabulous mixture of flowers and vegetables growing in the cottage gardens and allotments in the Spring and Summer.

What you need

Large Corsage
8" diameter

15cms (6") WOF of 3 different fabrics

Button

Embroidery thread

Small Corsage
5" diameter

10cms (4") WOF of 2 different fabrics

Button

Embroidery thread

Cutting Recipe

Large Corsage

From each fabric cut 2 squares 6" x 6" and 2 squares 4" x 4"

From one of these fabrics also cut 2 circles, see page 58 for template A

Small Corsage

From each fabric cut 3 squares 4" x 4"

From one of these fabrics cut a template A and from a different fabric cut a template B, see page 58 for template.

How to make it

Large Corsage

Take the 6" squares and fold in half on the diagonal. Fold in half again and pin each one in the middle to secure. **Use the photo as a guide for colour placement of the petals.**

Using a double thread take one triangle and using a running stitch sew along the long edge.

Gather in to form a petal and secure with a back stitch. **Do not cut the thread.**

Continue using the same thread, take the next triangle and repeat the process.

Continue until all 6 petals have been gathered and stitch the last two together to form a circle.

You have now completed the first layer of petals.

Repeat the process with the 4" squares these make up the second layer of petals.

Take one of the circles and sew a running stitch close to the edge, gather to form a Yo-Yo (Suffolk puff).

To assemble the corsage lay the remaining circle right side facing down. Position the first layer of petals on top of the circle. Position the second layer of petals on top of these and pin all 3 layers together.

Sew through all 3 layers to hold them together, hiding stitches in the folds.

Add the Yo-Yo to the top and secure with the button.

Small Corsage

This is made in the same way as the large corsage but without the first layer of petals.

Use the large circle template A for the Yo-Yo and the small circle for the backing.

These delightful corsages are very fashionable again today. They are ideal to embellish and decorate bags, cushions, frames, soft furnishings.

The School & The Little 'uns

Wor teacher made school so much fun, there were plenty of games to be played

Chalked squares for hopscotch were all over the place, when you got good at hopscotch, you went on to Hitchy Dabbers.

Anyways you had to throw the dabber into a square, you then had to hop on one leg and kick the dabber into each numbered square without it landing on a line. The dabber was the bottom of a jar or something like that; we kept them in our pockets so we could play the game at any time.

florrie

Arabella Jane & her Peggies

They were special days

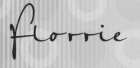

We went to chapel three times a day on Sunday, in those days we had to say a piece, it was poetry and we had to learn it and we could recite it to the parents and get a little prize. They were special days.

florrie

Arabella is dressed in her Sunday best, proudly holding her Peg Dolls in her arms. She is a smart doll in a full skirted dress inspired by the prominence of The Chapel.

What you need

For Arabella Jane

Calico 25cms (10")

Patterned fabric for feet Fat 8th

Bodice/Sleeves fabric 20cms (8")

Skirt fabric 25cms (10")

Petticoat 30cm (12")

Dolls hair

Ribbon 20cms (8")

Button

Toy filling

Freezer paper

Pigma Pen

For the Peggies

3 x Dolly Pegs

3 x Assorted fabrics 9" x 6"

3 buttons

Lace

Glue Gel

Freezer paper

Finished Size: 18" high approx

How to make it

This is a combination of 2 projects once both are complete you will be able to present the Peggies to Arabella Jane.

Arabella Jane

The body

Fold the calico in half with RST, make freezer paper templates of the hands and body page 58.

Using the templates as a guide, sew the hands and body, leaving openings as indicated on the pattern pieces.

Fold the feet fabric in half with RST. Make freezer paper template of the feet on page 58 and sew as per the hands & body.

Using pinking shears cut out the pieces and turn through.

Make a paper bag bottom on the body. See Work Basket.

Stuff the feet, hands and body to the lines indicated on the pattern. Sew openings closed.

To make the Petticoat

Cut one piece of fabric 15"x8". On one long side make a small hem and sew in place, this is the top of the petticoat.

Cut a piece of fabric 3" x 42" and fold in half lengthways WST and iron. Gather the raw edges until it measures 15".

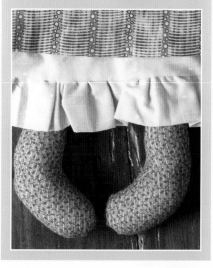

Continued

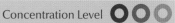

Arabella Jane & her Peggies

Best in Town

Have you met

  Miss Arabella Jane

Most people do declare

Her peg dolls

  are the best in town

Some say beyond compare

Betty

Pin this piece to the bottom of the petticoat RST and sew in place. Fold petticoat in half RST and sew the side seam. Position this seam to the back.

Now place the feet into the bottom of the petticoat so the feet show.

Sew the feet into place above the frill. Put the petticoat onto the waist of the doll and sew securely in place. **See photo on page 44.**

Arabella's Dress

From the bodice fabric cut 2 pieces 3" x 12½". With RST sew along one long edge leaving a 3½" gap in the centre for the head.

Cut 2 pieces 2½" x 12" for the frills of the sleeves.

Fold each of these pieces in half lengthways WST press and gather along each long edge until they are the same size as the sleeve edges (5½" approx). Pin frills onto the sleeve edges RST and sew in place.

Take the skirt fabric and cut in half on the long side, you will now have 2 pieces 9" x 21" approximately. Gather the top of each long piece with a small running stitch until they measure 6½" each.

Pin one of the skirt pieces RST to the front of the bodice, in the centre and repeat for the back and sew in place.

With RST, starting at the bottom of the sleeves sew the side seams and turn through.

Position the hands into the sleeves, leave the hands showing and sew in place above the frill.

Fit the dress to the body and then hem the dress ensuring the petticoat is showing.

Add a button to the neck to secure the dress in place.

Pull the hands together. **See photo on page 44.** Sew the frills at the bottom of the sleeves together at one point to keep them in place.

The Hair

It is better to do the hair before the face. Put 2 pins in head for the eye placement.

Cut the doll hair into 18" lengths and then fold these in half. Starting at the seam on the top of the head create a fringe by allowing the folded loops to fall over the face. Sew in place. **See main photo.**

Continue sewing the hair in rows until the back of the head is covered. Arabella has long hair trim to desired length. Add a bow **see photo**. Cut the loops of the fringe and trim if necessary.

Using a Pigma Pen draw in eyes, and use blusher for rosy cheek features.

The Peggies

For each doll cut circle templates A & B, on page 58.

Using pinking shears cut an A & B circle from fabric.

Cut a small slit in circle B and then Fold in half WST and sew. This is the bodice. **See Photo.**

Cut a small slit into the centre of circle A and push the peg through to form a skirt. **See Photo.**

Put bodice over the head.

Bring the edges of the bodice to the front and secure with a button. **See photo.**

Make a small bow from the lace and glue on head.

Repeat for other Peggies

Arabella Jane will be so happy when her Peggies are slipped under her arms so she can keep a mothering eye on them.

School Stitchery

Playing Out

After school we played out, we would come home, have wa tea and go out to play in the streets with skippy ropes or play games like hitchy dabbers.

I can remember coming home and we had like a back end, a little kitchen and of course a big room with everything in there. We had what they call a long settle and it went along the wall to the fire place and everybody that come in used to sit there because it was lovely and warm and I can remember playing schools then with a stick and I used to hit a long settle because they were being naughty.

florrie

Beamish School is full of history and games from the past.

We loved the Boolers', they were great fun. Using archive photographs and costumes from the period we have produced a charming stitchery encapsulating these elements. The framing was inspired by the old chalk boards in the classrooms.

What you need

Background fabric Fat quarter	Weaveline Fat quarter (optional)
Border fabric 10cms (4")	Red stranded cotton

Finished Size: 16" x 16" approx

Cutting recipe

Border fabric cut two x 2" strips

How to make

Trace the stitchery pattern on page 61 onto the centre of the background fabric.

Place the weave line on the back.

All stitching is completed with 2 strands of embroidery thread.

When completed trim the stitchery to 14" x 14" then add the borders.

We had our stitchery framed to look like an old chalkboard.

See the Work Basket for a guide to the stitches we have used.

This stitchery looks lovely made into a simple wall hanging, cushion or used as a bag panel. We have worked the stitchery in red thread but why not try other colours for a different effect?

Merry Go Round Bunting

The Merry Go Round

Can you hear that
*   wonderful sound?*
It's finally here
*   The Merry Go Round*
With a shiny new penny
*   the little 'uns wait*
For the man in the box
*   to open the gate*

They rush excitedly
*   to the ride*
Brother and sister
*   side by side*
Some horses are grey
*   some horses are white*
They really are a
*   beautiful sight*

Betty

We have again used the hexagonal shape from the shelving for this project creating an unusual bunting with the Merry Go Round horses from the stitchery added as an appliqué.

What you need to make 10 hexagons

Background fabric 50cms (20")	Backing fabric 50cms (20")
Scraps of fabric for Appliqué	Heat 'n' Bond Ultra
Wadding 1m (40")	Crocheted Lace or Large Ric Rac 140" length

Finished Size of one hexagon: 8" x 9" approx

How to make it

Make a freezer paper template using the hexagon on page 55.

Cut 10 hexagons from the background and backing fabrics.

Cut 10 hexagons from the wadding; make them slightly smaller than the fabric hexagons.

Trace a horse from the stitchery pattern on page 62 onto the Heat 'n' Bond Ultra.

Fuse a horse onto the centre of each of the background fabrics, for placement **see photo.**

Layer up the hexagons and stitch as desired.

To prevent fraying pink around the edge of each piece.

Starting at the centre of the lace pin each hexagon into place, evenly spacing them, and sew to secure. **See main photo.**

See hints in the Work Basket for the appliqué.

This is an ideal project to use up your scrap fabrics. Florrie used up her scraps from the Pitfield Street Quilt for her backing fabrics.

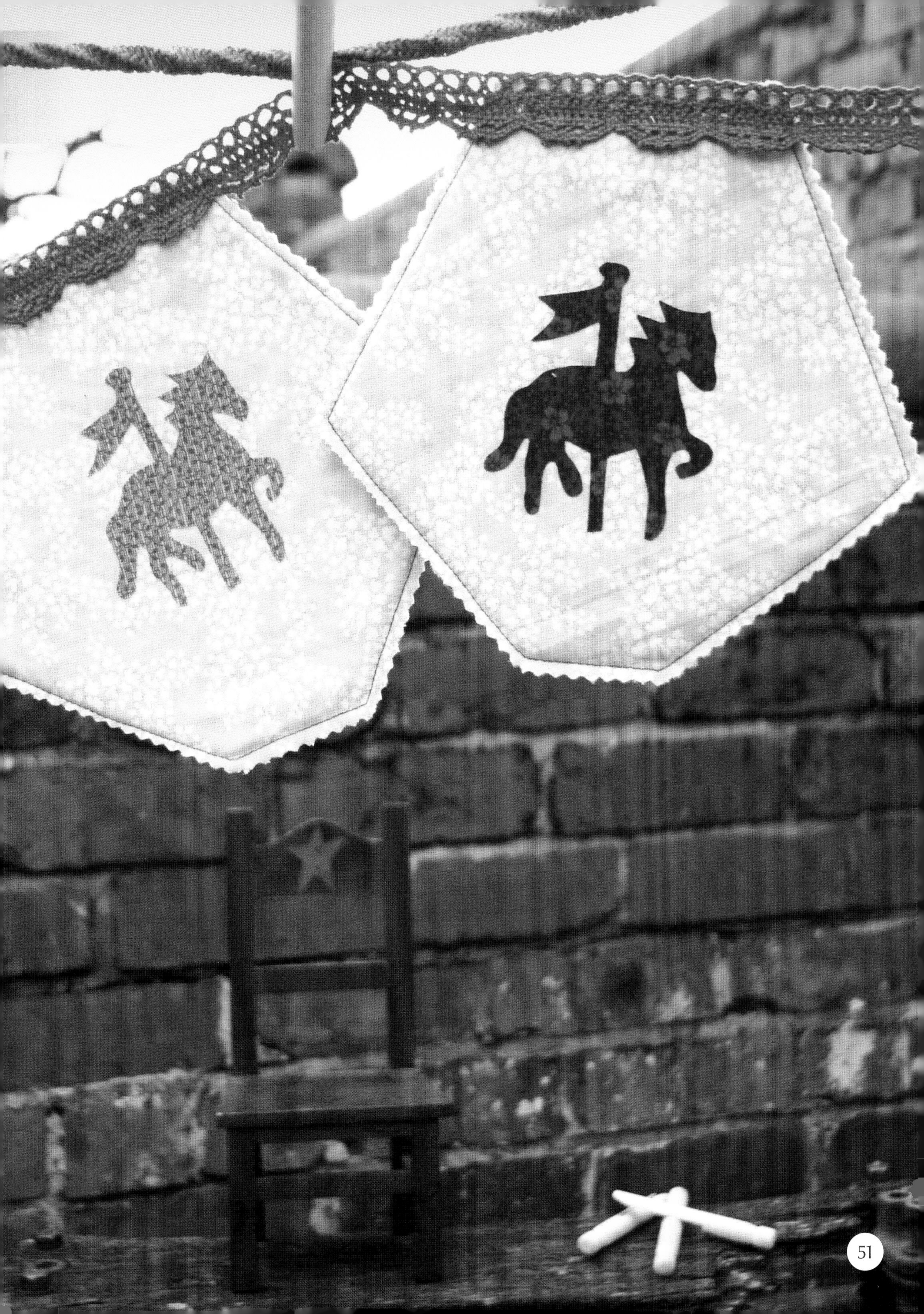

Florrie & Betty's Work Basket

All kinds of lovely things are hidden away in Florrie & Betty's Work Basket, it is always a treat to explore

Me mother used to say watch your fingers with that needle, I've a large collection of thimbles now

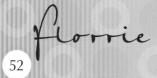

CONFUSION ARISES OVER STITCHES

A local member of The Women's Institute would like put the record straight and has said, "She knows her french knots from her back stitches and can point out a running stitch at 20 yards".

Allegations of a scant disregard were raised when it was found that incorrect stitches were used on a current 'stitchery pattern'. It was also alleged that there was also stitching taking place under the influence of sherry.

A statement was later released from The Women's Institute stating sherry is used for medicinal purposes only.

FRENCH KNOT DIAGRAM

BACK STITCH DIAGRAM

RUNNING STITCH DIAGRAM

CHILDREN DAY TRI COAST

Local children w a day trip to Wh thanks to the ger local dignitaries.

The children trav train supervised Florrie and Miss Packed lunches w provided and gre was had by all!

Norman, a seven old boy told repo 'I've had the bes me life, we've pl the beach and pa the sea, me mam believe what I've The best bit was had a bag of wil a lovely polished

CYCLE RI
RECORD 7

Young cyclists D and Sid complete regular bike ride Seaton Sluice to in record breakin Dennis has since treatment for a b received along th and Sid is said to looking for extra for his saddle be next outing.

On her recent vis to Whitley Bay, Betty was seen t egging on the ric paying particular to Sid. A passerb Sid's tight shorts have had someth to do with it.

Templates

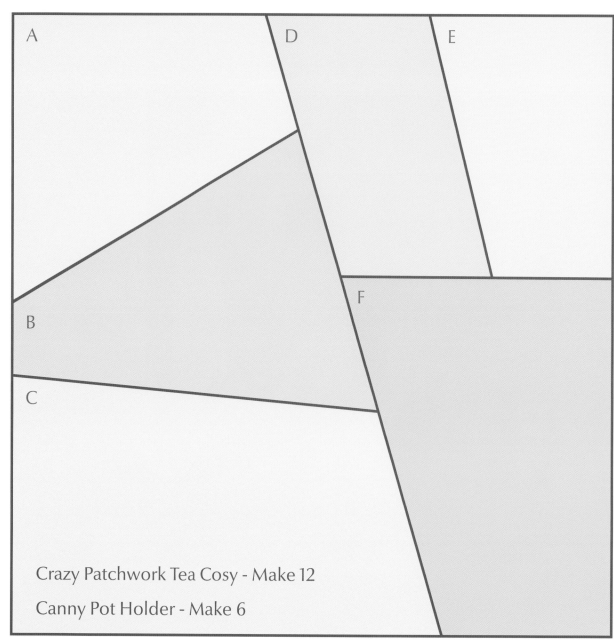

A

D

E

B

C

F

Crazy Patchwork Tea Cosy - Make 12

Canny Pot Holder - Make 6

Slang Hangings - Canny

adjective
NE English
pleasant/nice

Sub cutting

In the cutting recipes we have given an instruction for the first cut of the fabric. The sub cut is the second cut from the same piece of fabric.

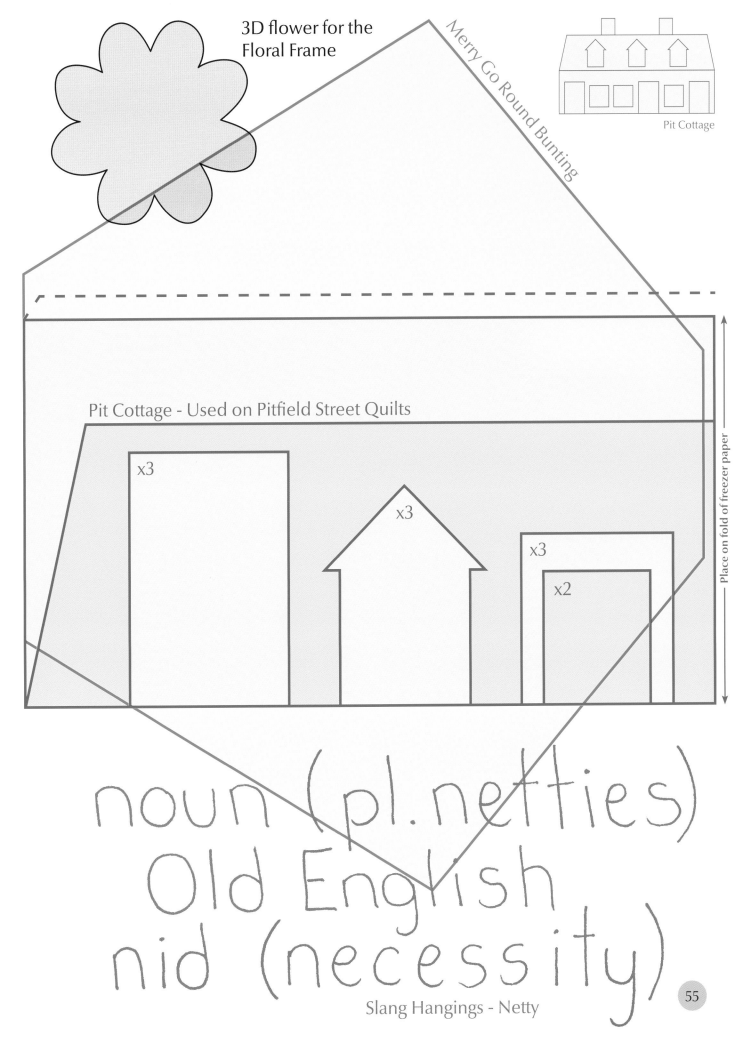

3D flower for the
Floral Frame

Pit Cottage

Pit Cottage - Used on Pitfield Street Quilts

x3

x3

x3

x2

Place on fold of freezer paper

noun (pl.netties)
Old English
nid (necessity).

Slang Hangings - Netty

Templates

Mother's Posh Bag

Pleats

Dart

Fusible Appliqué

Our preferred fusible paper is Heat 'n' Bond. The Lite needs to be sewn in place the Ultra does not.

Trace the design onto the smooth side of fusible paper. Cut out roughly

(so you can still see your drawn line).

Fuse to the reverse of the fabric, using a hot iron, no steam. Do not overheat as it reverses the process.

Cut out the design on the line, and peel off the backing paper. Position onto the background fabric and fuse in place with the iron as before.

Paper Bag bottom

This makes the base stand flat. It can be used during bag making or in our case when we made the doll.

Pull the back and the front apart. Align the side seams with the bottom seam and also align the edges of the squares. Stitch seam across the square, repeat on the other side.

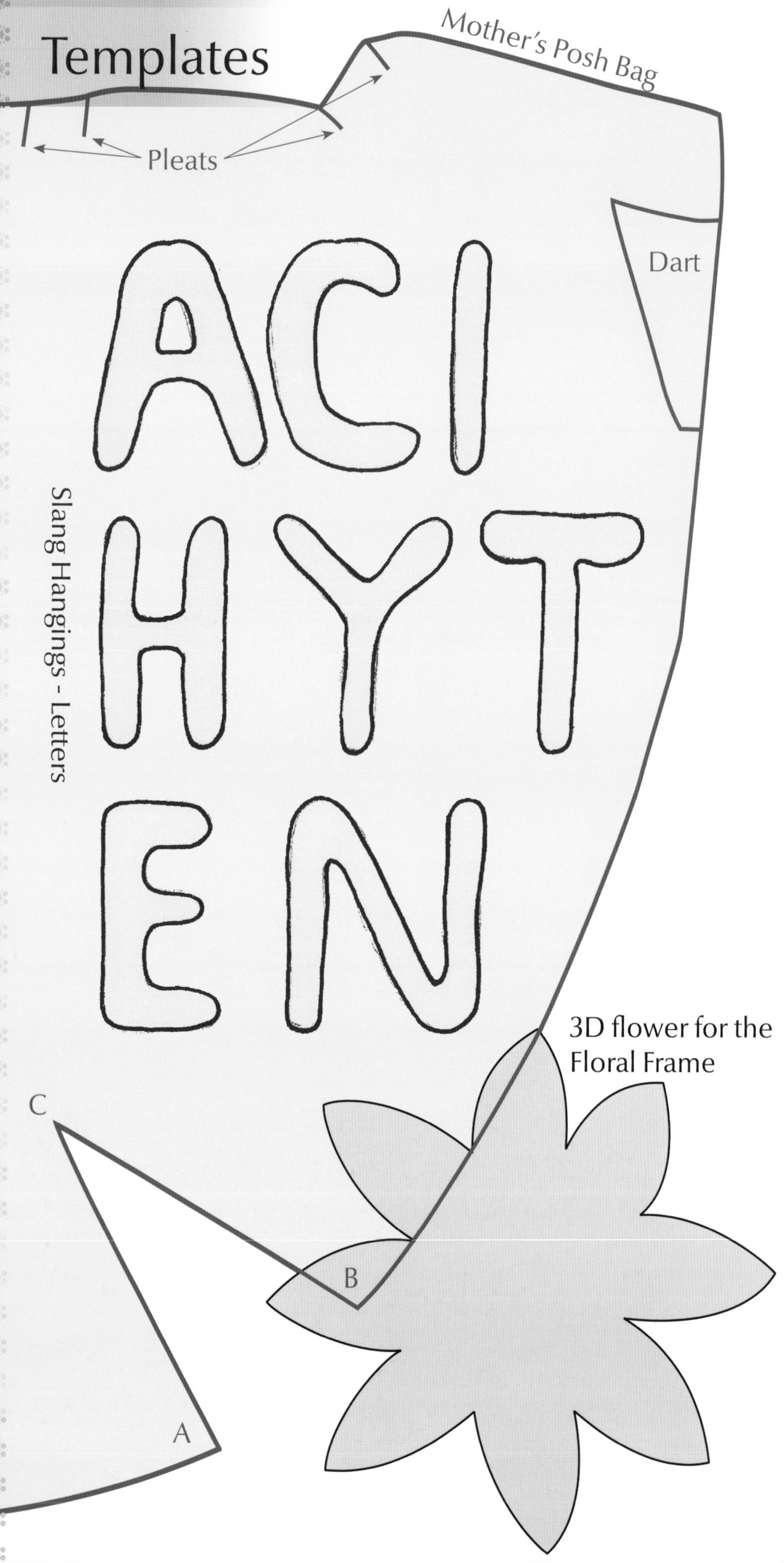

Slang Hangings - Letters

A C I
H Y T
E N

Place on fold of freezer paper

C

A

B

3D flower for the Floral Frame

Church - Used on Pitfield Street Quilts

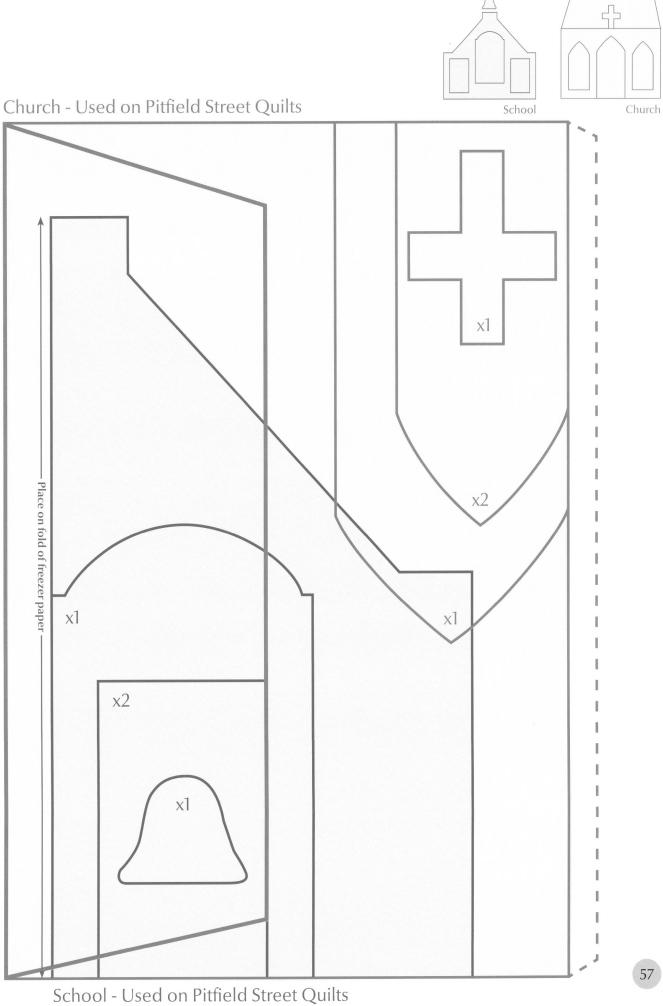

Place on fold of freezer paper

x1

x2

x1

x1

x2

x1

School

Church

School - Used on Pitfield Street Quilts

Templates

Yo-Yo's

(Suffolk puffs) Trace the circle template; we have used several in the book. Using a matching thread sew a gathering stitch approximately ¼" from the outer edge. Pull to gather, and secure the centre with a small stitch. We use linen thread for gathering as it is stronger. Do not worry if your centres are not perfect, add a button. An alternative to this method would be to use a 'Clover' Yo-Yo maker

Quilting

Quilting stitches hold all three layers together and can create texture.

You can hand or machine quilt. If using a sewing machine increase the stitch length. Some machines have a setting which will automatically do this.

If sewing by hand use a quilting needle or between and do a running stitch through all 3 layers. Do not worry about doing small stitches it is better that all your stitches are the same length. The more you do the better you will get. Betty prefers to use a Quilt hoop available from your local quilting shop.

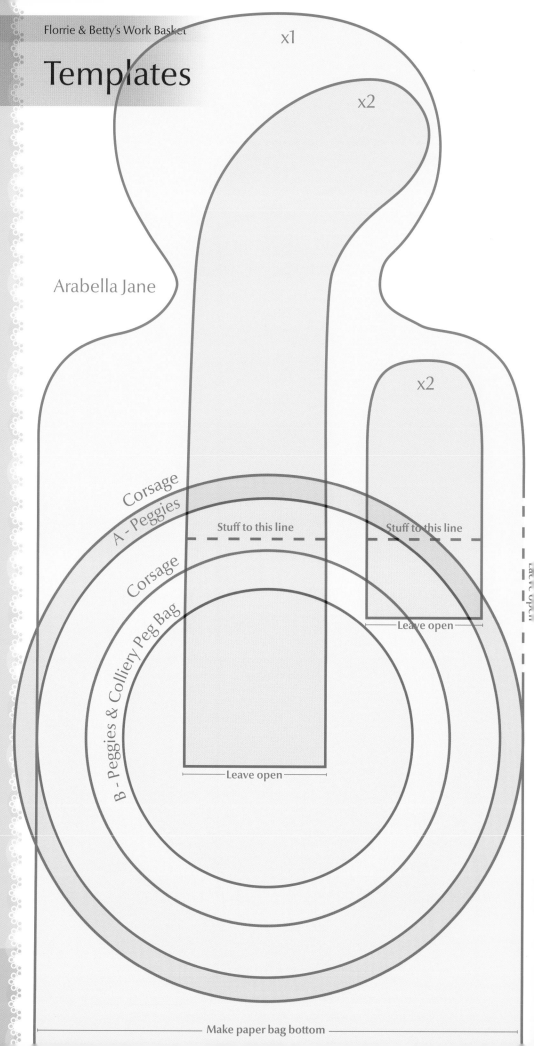

x1

x2

x2

Arabella Jane

Corsage

A - Peggies

Corsage

B - Peggies & Colliery Peg Bag

Stuff to this line

Stuff to this line

Leave open

Leave open

Make paper bag bottom

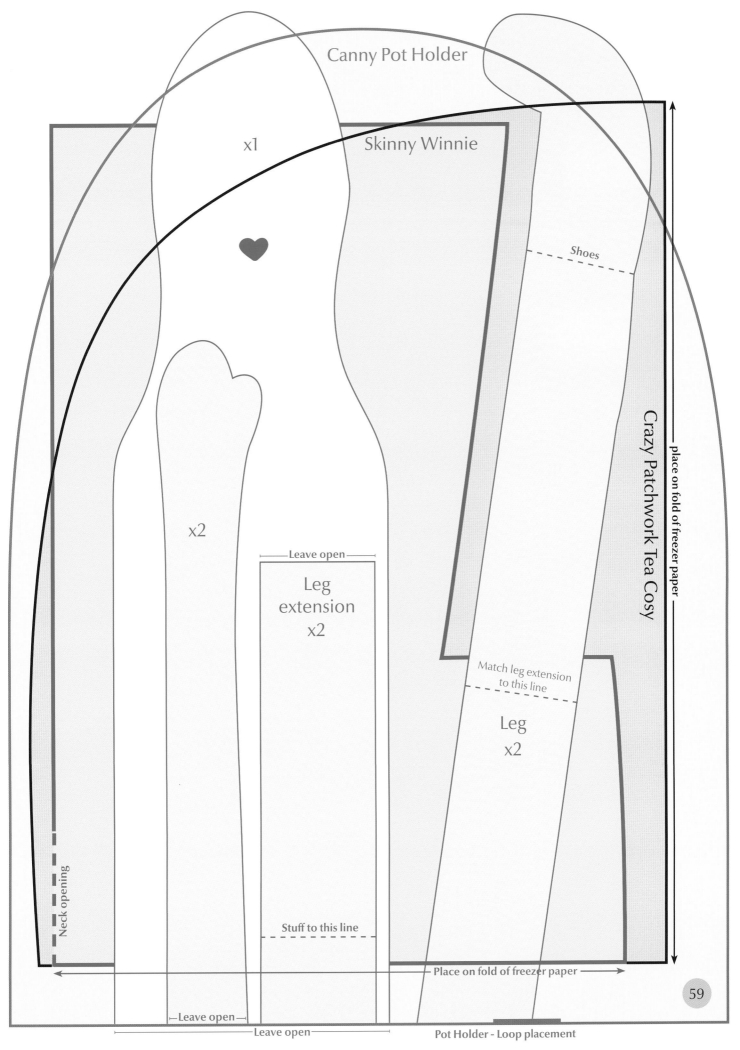

Canny Pot Holder

x1

Skinny Winnie

Shoes

place on fold of freezer paper

Crazy Patchwork Tea Cosy

x2

Leave open

Leg
extension
x2

Match leg extension
to this line

Leg
x2

Neck opening

Stuff to this line

Leave open

Place on fold of freezer paper

Leave open

Leave open

Pot Holder - Loop placement

Templates

Layering up a Quilt

The quilt sandwich is made up of 3 layers, the quilt top, wadding & backing fabric. Ensure the wadding and backing fabric is approximately 3" larger on each side than the quilt top.

Lay the fabric on a flat surface and lay the wadding on top. Smooth out any wrinkles. Lay the quilt top in the centre. Baste the 3 layers in a grid. You are now ready to start quilting.

Colliery Peg Bag

C - Complete shape

A

B

Place on fold of freezer paper

Proggy Flower - Used on Proggy Tea Pot Stand

Tab placement

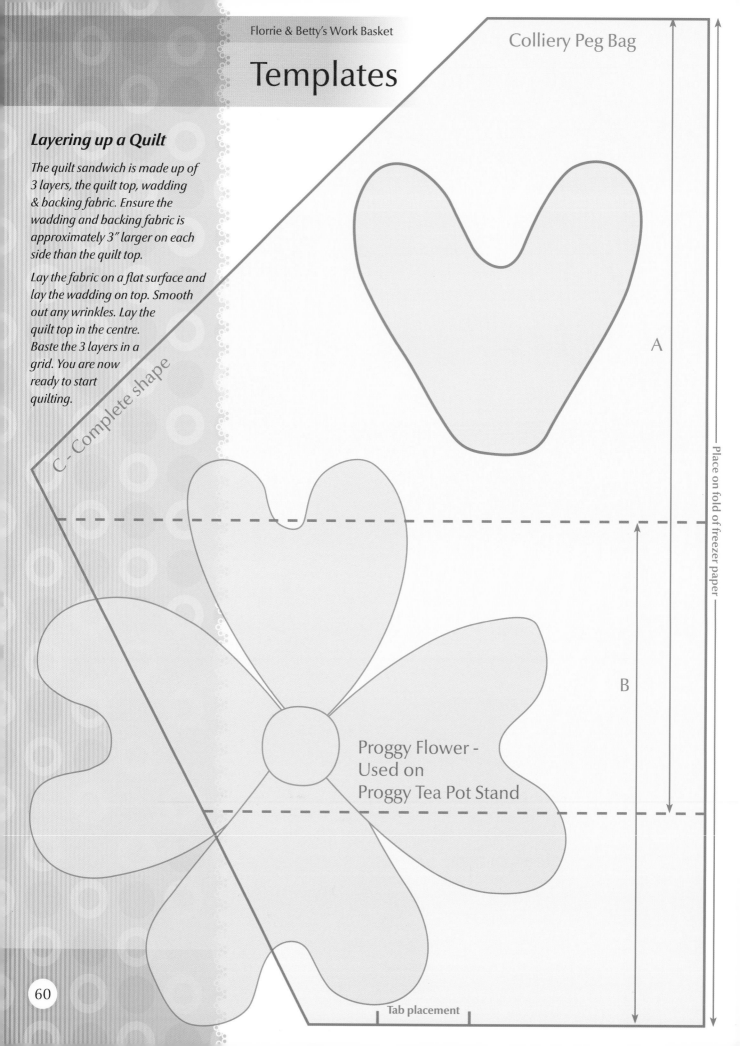

noun (pl.hinnies)
NE English
term of endearment

Slang Hangings - Hinny

Templates

Merry Go
Round Cushion

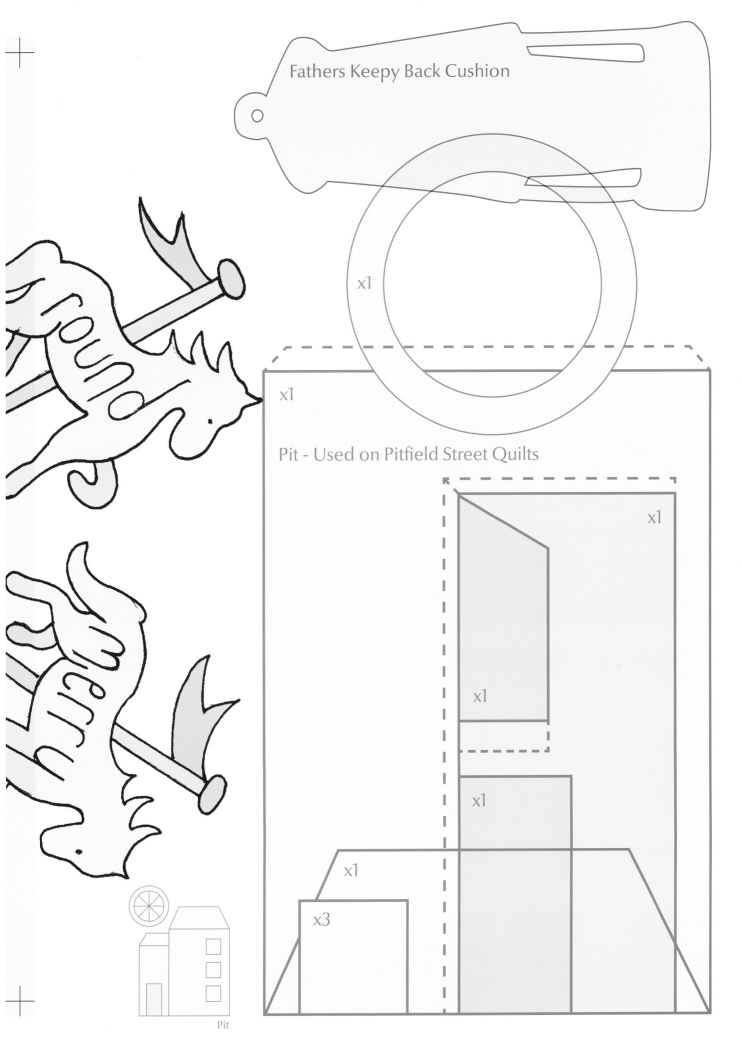

Fathers Keepy Back Cushion

x1

Pit - Used on Pitfield Street Quilts

x1

x1

x1

x1

x1

x3

Pit

About the materials used...

Having fun along the way

An idea born out of one or quite a few G&T's had us thinking about a little trip and now we have set off on a fabulous journey. Friends new and old are welcome to come along, smiles and laughter all the way.

For this our first book we have used a range of fabrics from Windham Fabrics.

Windham Fabrics continually produce new ranges which would fit equally as well with all of the projects.

Alternatively you could pick something completely different. Why not try a quilt in pastels, brights or batiks and Arabella looks fab dressed in any colour.

Thank you to Windham Fabrics for endorsing this book and encouraging us to continue with more of the same. A big thank you to Laura who has helped us on our journey.

All of the other products used throughout the book for example threads and haberdashery have been from Coats UK. Again a big thank you for their endorsement and help.

Marvellous!

Florrie & Betty

We Raise our Glasses to....

Beamish Museum
For a fantastic setting.
In particular to Jacki for all her help.

Big River Photography
Duncan and Jan for lovely pics and entering into the spirit of things.

Black Horse Beamish
Refreshments, nibbles & G&T's in the sun.

We lift them again to...
Terry Pinnegar Photography for additional images (pages 26, 30 and 50)

A huge 'Hipp Hipp Hooray' to...
Betty Garland
Annette Robinson
Margaret Urwin

Florrie and Betty would also like to thank all the canny lads & lasses who have supported them.